100

tips for a

Happy Baby

100

tips for a
Happy Baby

Alison Mackonochie

BARRON'S

First English edition for North America published by
Barron's Educational Series, Inc., 2004

First published by **MQ Publications Limited**
12 The Ivories, 6-8 Northampton Street, London, N1 2HY, England
website: www.mqpublications.com

Illustrations copyright © Elizabeth Harbour 2004
SERIES EDITOR: Abi Rowsell
DESIGN: Bet Ayer

All inquiries should be addressed to:
Barron's Educational Series, Inc.
250 Wireless Boulevard
Hauppauge, New York 11788
http://www.barronseduc.com

International Standard Book No. 0-7641-5762-0

Library of Congress Catalog Card No. 2003112710

Printed and bound in China

9 8 7 6 5 4 3 2 1

This book is intended as an informational guide only and is not to be used as a
substitute for professional medical care or treatment. Neither the author nor the
publisher can be held responsible for any damage, injury, or otherwise resulting
from the use of the information in this book.

Contents

Introduction

Being a parent can be both exciting and very rewarding. It's wonderful to watch your baby's development from a tiny, helpless little being into a sturdy, adventurous, and confident toddler. But it can be a time of anxiety, too, especially if you are a first-time parent, with natural concerns about your baby's day-to-day care and general well-being. This is where this book

 will help you. Packed with information, *100 Tips for a Happy Baby* draws on a wealth of experience to bring you easy-to-follow guidelines that will take you through the first year of your baby's life.

If you are worried about cradle cap, want to know about buying secondhand equipment, or plan to take your baby traveling, you'll find answers to your questions in Chapter 1, "Baby Care." Full of tried and tested advice on how to take care of your baby, it covers a wide variety of topics. Chapter 2, "Feeding without Fuss," gives tips for successful breast- and bottle-feeding, as well as the best ways to introduce your baby to solids. "Quiet Nights," Chapter 3, is a must if you're experiencing sleepless nights because it gives foolproof remedies that help to change a wakeful baby into a peaceful sleeper. Chapter 4, "Fun and Games," gives ways to stimulate and entertain your baby while also helping him develop skills such as spatial awareness, color recognition, and use of language. Finally, because feeling happy yourself goes a long way toward having a happy baby, "Happy Mom, Happy Baby," shows how to make the most of your role as a parent and enjoy this special time. Follow our expert advice and you'll be a happy parent with a happy baby!

Baby Care

1

Coping with cradle cap

Although unsightly, cradle cap doesn't usually cause your baby any discomfort. You can help loosen the scales by gently rubbing small amounts of baby oil or warmed olive oil into the affected area and leaving it on overnight. In the morning, use a soft bristle brush to remove any loose flakes. If it doesn't clear up or gets worse, consult your healthcare provider.

2

Hair washing without tears

Always use a hypoallergenic, nonsting shampoo and be very careful not to splash your baby's face or get shampoo in her eyes. You could try using a specially designed plastic shampoo shield that fits around the hairline and stops water and shampoo from getting onto the face.

3

Taking care of your baby's teeth

It's never too early to start brushing your baby's teeth. As soon as those first "milk" teeth appear, gently wipe the gums and teeth with a clean, soft, damp cloth at bedtime. Once six or more teeth have come through, start using a soft baby toothbrush and a pea-sized

 amount of baby toothpaste. Brush your baby's teeth every morning and evening. Allow him to play with his toothbrush while you brush your own teeth. By making toothbrushing fun now, you will be encouraging good oral hygiene, and that will help to prevent tooth decay in the future.

4

Making the "big" bath a breeze

Young babies don't usually like being immersed in water, so being bathed in the family tub can be frightening for your baby—and for you. You can help overcome your baby's fears by placing her in a specially designed bath support that will make her feel safe and secure in the water, or by getting into the bath with her. Whatever choice you make, *never* leave your baby alone in the bath, even for one second.

5

Natural odors

Your baby learns a lot about his environment through smell. He recognizes you by your smell and uses the smell of your breast milk to locate the breast when he's hungry. Products with strong fragrances interfere with this natural process, so avoid using highly scented cosmetics and toiletries.

6

Choosing easy-care fabrics

Your baby's clothes will need frequent washing—a newborn baby may need a complete change three or four times a day—so make life easy for yourself by choosing garments made from hard-wearing, easy-care fabrics. Avoid rough fabrics such as denim and look for soft, natural fibers such as cotton flannel or cotton fleece, which will be soft against your baby's delicate skin. Check the washing instructions before you buy to make sure the items are machine-washable and require minimal ironing. The less time you need to spend washing and ironing, the more time you will have for fun and games with your baby.

7

Disposables all wrapped up

Disposable diapers are easy to use and convenient, especially when you are away from home. But disposing of them isn't so easy, and many end up in the kitchen trash, leading to unsavory smells and hygiene problems. A better answer could be to invest in a unit that seals each used diaper in a film wrapper so that there is no smell, and that stores several days' worth at a time. Once the unit is full, the diapers can be carried to the outdoor trash can.

8

Natural solutions

If you use cloth diapers, it is important to wash them in boiling hot water, which sterilizes them and protects your baby's delicate skin from infection. Or you can use a sterilizing solution. Although there are proprietary sterilizing solutions on the market, you can also make your own by adding five drops of tea tree oil to a gallon of water. Alternatively, try one-half to one cup of white distilled vinegar, which will also act as a fabric softener. Avoid using standard detergents and bleach when you wash the diapers, because residues left on a diaper can irritate your baby's skin. Some fabric softeners make diapers less absorbent, so avoid them.

9

Keep sore bottoms at bay

Bacteria from your baby's stools react with urine to create an
alkaline irritant that can give your baby diaper rash. To prevent this,
change your baby's diaper frequently so his skin isn't exposed to a dirty
or wet diaper for long. This is especially important if you use highly

absorbent disposable diapers. If you use fabric diapers, make
sure that they are thoroughly sterilized before each use.

10

On the mat

Use a changing mat when you change your baby—it helps to keep the
mess under control. And, if the room is warm, let your baby lie on the
mat and kick without a diaper for a few minutes. He will enjoy the
freedom and the air will be good for his skin.

11

Treating diaper rash

If diaper rash develops, you can help speed the healing

process by cleaning the area thoroughly at each change and

allowing the skin to air-dry. Apply a specially formulated cream to the

rash or, if you prefer something more natural, use calendula (marigold)

cream or chamomile and lavender essential oils to soothe the affected

area. Add one drop of each oil to a bowl of warm water and use a

cotton ball to wipe your baby's bottom with the solution.

12

Out and about

When taking your baby out, you'll want to be sure that he is comfortable and safe. Think about practical matters, too. For example, a traditional baby carriage gives a good firm ride and protects against drafts and car fumes. However, it is impractical if you use public transportation or have a small car. If most of your journeys are on foot, your baby may be happier in a well-padded stroller with maneuverable wheels. Many strollers have an optional bed so you can use them for a newborn. Or choose an all-in-one travel carrier with an integral car seat, which enables you to carry your sleeping baby indoors from the car without disturbing him. This is probably the best choice if a car is your main mode of transport. When using any type of car seat, it is important to check that it is attached properly. A two-in-one carriage converts from a traditional design, where your baby lies flat, to a rear/forward-facing stroller for

an older baby. A multiposition stroller with a rigid
back support can be used from birth, but
umbrella-type folding strollers shouldn't be
used until the baby is at least three
months old. Whatever you decide on,
remember to harness your baby
securely into it. If you use a
raincover, make sure your
child isn't too warm.

19

13

Taking to the air

If you are planning a long flight, ask for a sky cot or bassinet when you reserve your seats. A sky cot is a hammock-style bed suitable for a young baby—usually under a year—that is placed in front of the bulkhead seats. These beds have size and weight restrictions; check their suitability when you talk to the airline. With your baby in a sky cot for at least part of the journey, you will both be more likely to get some rest. On take off and landing, you must hold the baby in your lap. Another option is to purchase a ticket for the infant; however, you must then use an approved infant seat.

14

Pressure changes

When you are flying, breast-feed your baby or offer a bottle or pacifier when you take off and land. Sucking helps prevent earaches caused by the changes in air pressure.

Travel documents

If you are taking your baby overseas, he will need travel documents just as you do, no matter how young he is. Your nationality determines whether or not he requires his own passport. Check about laws and regulations with your travel agent, airline, or passport office before you travel.

16

Baby carriers

Your newborn will love being carried snuggled up against your front, no matter if you're at home or in the supermarket. Buy a carrier with a head support that can be removed once your baby gains head control. Always try before you buy to ensure that you can get the carrier off and on yourself, without help. At about six months, your baby will enjoy sitting in a carrier on your back and watching the world go by. A carrier is also ideal if you take long walks because it is so much easier to manage than a stroller.

17

Beating boredom in the car

When traveling in the car when your baby is older, keep a bag of toys on hand. A toy with a suction cup that sticks to the back of the seat in front of her is very practical—she can't drop it. If possible, attach to the seat a car bag that contains a number of different toys. Make these special; let your baby play with them only in the car.

18

Travel safely

A car seat is one of the most important pieces of baby equipment—the correct kind of restraint can protect your baby if you stop suddenly or have an accident. Car seats are required to be placed in the back seat. Infants—and, in general, children under twelve—can be harmed by front-seat airbags. Most important, always get professional help with fitting your chosen car seat. Research shows that a surprisingly high percentage of baby car seats are installed incorrectly. Always buy a seat that meets safety standards, and always buy new, not secondhand.

Before you buy, check the following guidelines:

- The seat should be suitable for use in your make of car.
- The 5-point harness should adjust easily.
- The covers should be removable and washable.
- The seat back should support your baby's head and you should check whether the seat reclines.

- The car seat must be suitable for your child's weight; weight is more important than age. Rear-facing baby seats are designed for babies from newborn up to 20 to 22 pounds (9 to 10 kg). At this age your baby's pelvis is still too soft to protect the internal organs properly. Using a rear-facing seat means that if there is an accident, any pressure is put on the child's back rather than his pelvis.

Check-ups

Your baby will have a number of scheduled well-baby checkups between the time she's born and when she starts school. These checks are designed to monitor how she is developing and also to screen for any medical abnormalities. The checks are important because medical professionals can pick up conditions that may not be obvious to you and can give treatment before the condition has affected your baby's progress. Don't miss any of these check-ups. Instead, use them as a time to discuss any concerns you may have about your baby's development.

Learning language

Your baby starts to communicate with you in the first weeks of life by making burbling noises. As he gets older, these gradually become coos and chuckles, often in response to attention from you. At about six months, he will begin to enjoy playing with different sounds; he'll babble and experiment with them for hours. You can help this early speech development by talking to him, repeating simple words, and encouraging him to copy you. Watch his facial expressions as he tries to imitate the sounds you make.

21

Stress-free dressing and undressing

Your baby may become fussy when you're dressing or undressing her. The faster you can change her clothes, the better. Make sure the room where you are changing her is warm and that your hands are, too. Stretch suits with snaps all the way down the front are quick and easy to put on; vests and tops with lap shoulders that easily stretch wide are also good choices. Two-piece outfits that expose only a part of her at a time may also cause less stress. Make plenty of soothing noises as you dress or undress your baby, and always finish with a big cuddle.

22

Buying secondhand

You can save yourself a lot of money by buying some of the more expensive items of baby equipment secondhand (except, of course a car seat). But remember that you won't have the same rights and safeguards as you do when buying new. Always inspect the equipment very carefully, be sure instructions are available for installation and use, if necessary, and buy it only if you are completely happy with its condition.

23

A place to sleep

A crib is the safest place for your baby to sleep, and it is important that you look out for certain safety guidelines before buying or borrowing one. Your baby's crib should never have:

- Any missing, loose, broken, or improperly installed screws, brackets or other hardware on the crib or the mattress support.
- More than $2\frac{3}{8}$ inches (6 cm) between the crib slats so a baby's head and body cannot slip between them.
- Corner posts more than $\frac{1}{16}$ inch (1.6 mm) above the end panels so there is no risk of a baby catching clothing and being strangled.
- Cut-out areas on the head or footboard that could trap a baby's head.
- Old, cracked or peeling paint (to prevent lead poisoning).
- Any splinters or rough edges.

If you are buying or borrowing a secondhand crib, a new mattress is a must. You can choose between mattresses made from foam or innersprings but fit is the important factor. Check that it fits snugly into the frame so there's no risk that your baby will be trapped between the frame and the edge of the mattress. For comfort, choose an innerspring mattress that's at least 4 inches (10 cm) thick, or contains at least 150 coils, or a foam mattress that's very dense. If you aren't confident of making the right choice, check with the crib manufacturer before you buy.

24

Helping the medicine to go down

If your baby is on liquid medication, you'll find it easier to give it to him in a syringe or dropper than on a teaspoon. Touch your baby's bottom lip to encourage him to open his mouth and then, leaning him back slightly, squeeze the medicine into his mouth. A very young baby may find it easier to take medicine from a dispenser shaped like a pacifier with a plunger. The baby can either suck the liquid from the nipple or you can press the plunger to give the medicine.

25

Knowing when she's ill

If your child is sick, take her temperature by placing a digital thermometer in her armpit, or use an ear thermometer. Both types have a beeper that tells you when the thermometer is ready. Liquid crystal strips that you place on your child's forehead are less stressful to use but also a lot less accurate. Don't use the old-fashioned mercury thermometers; they aren't safe enough for a baby.

Getting the temperature right

Your baby isn't able to control his body temperature as accurately as you

can, so it's up to you to make sure that he doesn't get too hot or too cold.

His body should feel warm to your touch but not damp or sweaty.

If his skin feels hot, he probably has too many clothes on.

However, you should also check for signs of fever. If his

hands and feet feel cold, he may not be warm

enough. Don't rely on him to cry to let you know

when he's cold—he may be

too busy conserving his energy

in order to maintain his body

temperature.

Feeding without Fuss

27

Testing the temperature

When you heat your baby's bottle, test the temperature of the milk before
giving it to him. Shake the bottle, then drip some milk onto the inside of
your wrist. It should feel neither too hot nor too cold on your skin. Not all
babies like their milk warm. Some prefer it unheated; if your baby likes
his bottle at room temperature, don't worry—it's safe for him to drink it
like this. But never give your baby a bottle straight from the refrigerator
because the cold could give him a tummy ache. Always throw away
any unfinished formula after feeding.

28

Enjoying skin-to-skin contact

The world can seem like a very strange and sometimes frightening place to a newborn. You are the most familiar thing in his life, so your baby needs close contact with you to feel secure. Cuddle him against your skin when you feed him, even if you are bottle-feeding.

29

Checking that the formula is flowing

If your bottle-fed baby seems as if he's sucking too hard or gets gassy from gulping milk too fast, check the milk flow. It should be about two or three drops a second—any more or less than that could cause a problem.

30

Burping your baby

If your baby gets very gassy while she's feeding, stop to burp her. When she's very young, sit her upright on your lap, support her neck and head, and gently rub her back. Once she has gained some control of her head, she may prefer to be burped when you hold her against your shoulder. If she doesn't burp after you've rubbed her back for thirty seconds or so, don't worry. Even if she doesn't need a burp, it's good for both of you to take a breather during feeding.

31

The perfect formula

When you use powdered formula, follow the
manufacturer's instructions precisely. Too rich a
formula can overload your baby's immature
digestive system, possibly causing long-term
damage, while too little leaves him hungry.

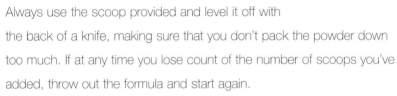

Always use the scoop provided and level it off with
the back of a knife, making sure that you don't pack the powder down
too much. If at any time you lose count of the number of scoops you've
added, throw out the formula and start again.

32

Sterilizing to protect your baby

Milk is the perfect breeding ground for harmful bacteria that could make your baby sick. Wash, rinse, and sterilize your baby's feeding equipment to reduce the risk of her getting an upset stomach or an infection. Choose from the three main sterilizing methods: chemical, steam, or microwave. If you are traveling or on vacation, sterilizing bottles may be a problem. It's easier then to use disposable bottles, which can be replaced at each feeding.

Healthy feeding

Exclusive breast-feeding is recommended until your baby is approximately six months old. During this time, water, juice, and other foods are generally not considered necessary. Once your baby reaches six months you will gradually need to introduce solids into his diet, although it is recommended that you also continue to breast-feed for at least 12 months. If you stop breast-feeding before he reaches a year, you will need to give him iron-fortified infant formula rather than cow's milk.

34

Controlling the mess

Use lots of newspapers or a large plastic mat under the high chair so you can easily clean up your baby's attempts at plastering the floor with the contents of his bowl. Keep a damp washcloth handy for wiping his hands and face, along with a supply of paper towels for mopping up spills. Roll up your baby's sleeves to keep them out of his food, and cover his shirt with a washable bib.

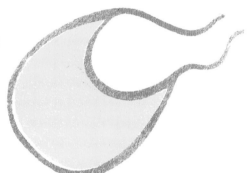

35

First weaning tools

An unbreakable baby bowl with a nonslip bottom keeps your baby from knocking it off her chair tray. Choose weaning spoons with long handles and small, shallow, soft bowls that won't hurt her mouth. Let her have one to experiment with while you feed her with the other. A plastic cup with a handle on each side lets her drink by herself. Always have two cups—one for home and one for going out. Finally, don't forget the bibs—they help to keep your baby's clothes at least reasonably clean.

36

Introducing first foods

When you first introduce your baby to solids, usually when he's between four and six months old, offer a small amount of a bland food such as baby cereal (rice or oat) mixed to a smooth consistency with breast or formula milk. This first food is just to get your baby used to the idea of different tastes and textures—his main nourishment is still coming from breast milk or formula. Put a small amount of food onto the tip of a weaning spoon. Be careful not to overload the spoon because too much food at a time will make him splutter. Sucking is a natural reflex for your baby; at first he will try to suck the food off the spoon. It will take him a while to learn how to get the food from the spoon into the back of his mouth so that he can swallow it. But once he's figured out how to do this, he will be ready for new tastes and will quickly learn how to handle lumpier textures. If your baby obviously doesn't like the taste of something, don't force him to eat it. Try another food and reintroduce the rejected food at a later stage.

37

Home cooking

It's perfectly alright to give your older baby home-cooked food as long as you haven't added sugar or salt, and it is not too high in fiber. Prepare the food in the normal way, but without adding salt or sugar. When it is cooked, remove a small portion for your baby, and add seasoning for yourself.

38

Food in a flash

Wash and dry an ice-cube tray or some empty yogurt containers so you can freeze simple first foods like fruit or vegetable puree in small amounts. You can defrost these baby-sized portions in a flash. Then, when hunger strikes, you don't need to keep your baby waiting.

39

High chairs, low chairs, or table seats?

Whichever design you buy, the right seat for your baby is an essential piece of equipment when you start to introduce him to solids. Make life simple for yourself and safe and hygienic for your baby by choosing a chair that is well padded, sturdy, and easy to clean. It should have an integral crotch strap and D-rings for a separate safety harness. Be careful when moving your child in or out of the chair, and never leave him alone in it, even if he's strapped in. Be careful also not to place the chair on a slippery or raised surface.

40

Easy does it

Although puréed fruit is a favorite first food, avoid using fruits with seeds, such as raspberries or strawberries—unless you have put them through a strainer—until your baby is at least six months old. Introduce foods one at a time, generally three to five days apart. If your baby has a reaction (a rash or diarrhea, for example), you'll know which food caused it. Avoid hard-boiled egg whites and foods containing gluten, such as wheat, rye, and barley, until your baby is a year old. Hold back on soft-boiled eggs until he reaches a year. Don't give honey until after his first birthday and avoid shellfish and nut products until he's two. Because of the risk of choking, don't give whole nuts to your child until he's at least five years old. You can use formula or breast milk on cereals and in sauces and puddings from the time your baby is six months old, but don't let him have cow's milk until he is at least a year old. Introduce other dairy products, such as cheese and yogurt, when he's a year old.

41

Making mealtime a family time

Your baby is a sociable little person who wants to be part of family mealtimes. When you all have a meal together, sit her at the table in her high chair so that she can join in the social interaction. She will soon discover that mealtimes are fun and this may help overcome any difficulties you have getting her to eat. And, even if you don't want to eat when she has her meal, don't use the time to rush about doing jobs. Sit with her and chat.

Eating out

Your baby will enjoy the novelty and excitement of eating out in a restaurant or cafe. Don't be worried about how he will behave. Select a family-friendly spot and relax. Remember to take his harness so that you can be sure he is safe in the high chair, and be prepared for him to get bored before you are finished. When this happens, try offering finger foods to keep him busy or provide a selection of toys from his car bag so he can play while you enjoy your meal.

Feeding on demand

Breast-feeding is not only the best and most natural way to feed your baby, it is also a great way of bonding with your newborn. Your milk is produced on a supply-and-demand basis, so letting your baby suckle whenever she's hungry helps to establish your milk supply. Allow her to feed for as long as she wants; your breasts need the stimulation of sucking to produce the right amount of milk. At first, she may want to feed every two hours or so, but she will soon settle into a more manageable routine.

Allergy alert

If allergies such as asthma and eczema run in your
family, delay giving your baby eggs, fish, wheat,
and cow's milk in any form until he's at least a
year old. Although the allergy may not affect your
baby, it's not worth taking the risk. Some babies react to
artificial food colorings and additives. Avoid these, too.

Quiet Nights

45

Sleeping safely

Research has shown that the incidents of Sudden Infant Death Syndrome (SIDS)—also known as crib death—have been substantially reduced by putting babies in the "feet-to-foot" position so that their feet reach the bottom of their crib. This way they can't wriggle down under the covers and get overheated. *Always place your baby on his back*, with the covers firmly tucked in no higher than shoulder level.

Alternatively, dress your baby in warm sleep clothes and place him on his back without any covers. Buy a new crib mattress, even if the crib is secondhand. The mattress must be firm and easy to clean; keep it well-aired, too. Never put your baby down to sleep in his crib with pillows, duvets, quilts, sheepskins, crib bumpers, or anything fluffy and soft—even stuffed

animals. Even if it's cold, don't be tempted to
warm up the crib with a hot-water bottle or an
electric blanket. It's best if your baby sleeps in your
room until he is at least six months old, or if you prefer to have
him sleep in his nursery, use a baby monitor. And *no one*
should smoke in the same room the baby is in.

46

The right temperature

Your baby can quickly become overheated, so it's important to make sure that the room in which she sleeps doesn't become too hot. Buy a room thermometer so you can maintain an ideal room temperature of 65°F (18°C).

47

Get the bedding right

Because of the risk to your baby from overheating, cover him with only a crib sheet and blankets in layers. Usually, a light blanket or just a blanket sleeper will do. Add or remove the blankets according to the temperature of the room. Remember that a doubled-over crib blanket counts as two layers.

Monitoring your baby at night

Check on your baby, even when he's asleep. A baby monitor allows you to relax, knowing that you will hear him if he needs you. Systems usually come with separate units for baby and parent and can be plugged in or battery-operated. Most monitors have a range of at least 30 feet (100 m), but check the reception before you use them. A sleep alarm with a sensor pad is more sophisticated; the pad, placed under the mattress, monitors your baby's movements and breathing. These sensors alert you if the baby makes no breathing movements for 20 seconds.

49

Swaddling a newborn

If your newborn involuntary jerks his limbs, it can keep him awake. Try wrapping him firmly in a soft, light crib blanket with his legs and arms tucked in. Lay him in the middle of the blanket with his arms by his sides. Gently pull one side of the blanket across his body, then pull the other side across and tuck it under him so that he is swaddled. Place him on his back to sleep. Check his temperature every hour or so to make sure that he doesn't get overheated.

50

Saying "Goodnight"

Although it may be tempting to cuddle your baby to sleep in your arms, you won't be doing him any favors. He needs to learn how to get to sleep on his own so that he knows how to do it again if he wakes in the night.

51

Creating a settling-
to-sleep routine

If you introduce a bedtime
routine when your baby is
about three months old, she
will understand that when it's
nighttime, it's time for a story, a cuddle,

and then sleep—not fun and games. Start by giving her a warm,
relaxing bath, then follow with a story, a feeding, and a cuddle
before you put her in her crib. She will enjoy listening to a musical
mobile or hearing you sing a lullaby as she drifts off to sleep.

Night-lights

Your baby may find it hard to settle at night simply because he doesn't like the dark. A night-light that gives off a soft, comforting glow often helps to calm his fears. Night-lights can vary tremendously. The simplest and cheapest versions plug into an electric outlet and glow in the dark. Some have small light bulbs. More complicated, expensive ones play music while the light projects images; some even light up when your baby cries.

53

Keeping the light out

If your baby is an early riser, line the nursery curtains with a thick "blackout" material to help her sleep longer on light mornings. Place some crib toys in the crib (nothing soft and fluffy), too, so that when she does eventually wake she has something to keep her amused for a while.

54

Dividing day and night

Help your baby understand the difference between nighttime and daytime sleep by keeping the crib for sleeping at night and a carriage, basket, or playpen for daytime naps. He will associate the crib with part of his bedtime routine and nighttime sleep.

55

Breaking the night-waking habit

If your baby's in the habit of waking in the night, breaking it won't be easy; this can take time and a lot of patience. However, you may discover that he only needs reassurance to go back to sleep. If you're sure that your baby is not hungry, wet, or uncomfortable, try gently talking to him for a few minutes while you stroke him. If he continues to cry, pick him up and soothe him. When he has calmed down, put him back into his crib with gentle words and keep stroking him until he's settled. Once he starts to drop off to sleep again leave him and go back to bed. If he starts to cry as soon as you leave him, try to wait for five minutes before going back to him. Don't pick him up, but stroke him again and talk soothingly. Keep this pattern up every five minutes for an hour, if necessary. You may want to enlist the help of your partner so that you can take turns at getting up during the night, or you may find it easier to cover alternate nights so that at least one of you gets a good night's sleep. Although you may both find the whole process emotionally and physically exhausting, it's worth remembering that it doesn't usually take more than a few nights to break the habit; then you will both be able to sleep well, every night.

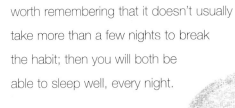

56

Pacifiers can be soothing

Sucking can be soothing to a wakeful baby, and a pacifier could be all she needs to get her off to sleep. It's best to give a pacifier only when your baby is going to sleep. Check that the one you use is in good condition, and don't forget to put it in the sterilizer before popping it in her mouth. If the pacifier falls out while she's asleep, she may start to wake. If that happens, you'll have to pop it back in for her.

57

Taking your baby into bed

In many cultures, taking your baby into bed is the accepted thing to do and it certainly makes sense when it comes to night feedings. But take some precautions when the baby's in your bed. Cover her with lightweight crib blankets rather than your blankets, and make sure your pillows and bedspread can't cover her head. Check that she can't fall out of bed and, if the bed is cramped, that you won't lie on her. Of course, if you or your partner have been drinking or if either of you is on medication, your baby will be safer in her own crib.

58

How much sleep does a baby need?

Your newborn has no concept of the difference between night and day and will sleep in short bursts for a total of up to 16 hours in every 24. As she gets older, her sleep pattern will gradually change so that she sleeps more at night and less during the day. By six months, your baby will be taking two to three naps a day and sleeping up to twelve hours at night. By your baby's first birthday, she will be sleeping one hour less than she did at six months. But all babies are individuals, so be prepared for your baby to be different.

59

Moving into the nursery

Choose a time to move your baby into her own room when she isn't having any other upsets in her life, such as being weaned or your returning to work. If she's already suffering from separation anxiety and doesn't like letting you out of her sight, wait until she's settled again before moving her out of your room.

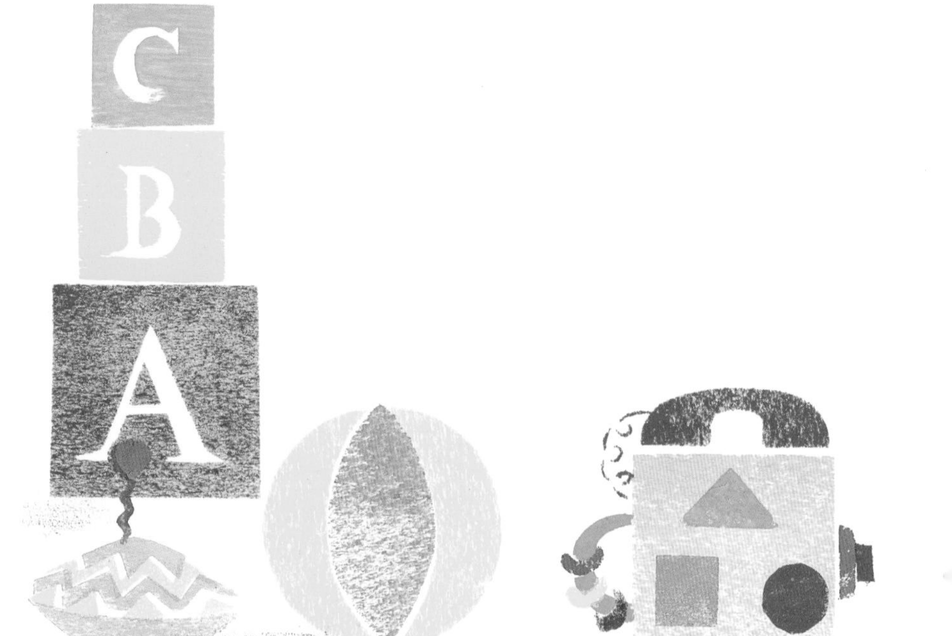
C
B
A

Fun and Games

60

Mirror, mirror . . .

Hang an unbreakable mirror in the crib where your baby can see her reflection, and encourage her to look at herself. She will get endless hours of enjoyment from studying her changing image. This also helps to develop her observation skills.

61

Imitating you

There is no doubt about it, you are your baby's favorite plaything. Even at three months old your baby will enjoy watching your facial expressions and will try to copy them. Hold him so that you have his attention, then stick out your tongue and make a noise. Watch your baby as he tries to imitate you.

Changing levels

Some research suggests that the more babies are encouraged to look at new objects, the higher they will score on intelligence  tests at the age of four. Move your baby to different rooms and different levels such as the floor, a chair, and the bed. Try looking at things from the same height as your baby and you'll see how being at a different level can make a big difference to what he sees. Encourage your baby to look at a number of objects in each room, and talk to him about what he can see.

63

Fun with colors

Put a brightly colored sock on one of your baby's feet so that he can see it when he kicks his legs. Once he's used to seeing the colored sock on this foot, change it to the other foot. Later, you can put the sock on his hand so that he can bring it close to his face and really concentrate on the color. Do this again the next day with a different colored sock, so that you gradually introduce your baby to a range of colors. As he gets older he will enjoy choosing which colors he likes best.

64

Shake, rattle, and roll

Your baby's hearing becomes more sophisticated as she gets older. By about three months, she will show an interest in sounds, even soft ones like your footsteps. You can help to develop her sound recognition at this age by encouraging her to listen and identify different noises. Try filling several small plastic containers with different objects such as dry beans, marbles, and rice. Fasten the lids securely with duct tape so she can't open them. Encourage her to shake or roll each container; she'll gradually learn to discriminate between the different noises.

65

Toys from the kitchen cupboard

Everyday household articles can give your child hours of entertainment and will help him learn about different shapes and textures. As your baby gets older, about nine months and up, try playing with these household toys. Banging a pan with a wooden spoon makes a noise as good as any drum. For water play, all you need are a dishpan containing a small amount of water, some plastic cups, a big spoon, and a sieve. A drawer or a cupboard that is safe for your baby to empty is absolutely absorbing. He may like to try playing with different-sized empty cardboard boxes, putting one inside another. Or help him stack the boxes, knock them down, and pile them up again. Look through empty paper towel or toilet paper cardboard rolls, use them for trumpets, or push smaller objects through them. By using your imagination and encouraging your child to explore the everyday items around him, you'll help him learn to use his imagination, too.

66

Laughing games

A good laugh makes us all feel better. Your baby is no exception; you'll treasure the times when you laugh together. Do silly things and see what appeals to her sense of humor. Try pretending to drink from her bottle, or eat her food. Build up a tower and knock it down, making silly noises as it falls. Play "boo" around the furniture or cover your face with a cloth and encourage your baby to pull it off, saying "peek-a-boo" as your eyes appear.

67

Talk, talk, talking to your baby

Listening to you and other people is the way your baby learns language. Talk to her about everyday things. Teach her word recognition by telling her what you are going to do before you do it. For example, say, "I am going to pick you up," and hold out your arms to her. After a while, you can drop the whole sentence and just say "up" as you hold out your arms. Your baby will soon reach out when she hears the word and understands its meaning.

68

Over, under, and through

As your baby becomes more mobile, at about nine months old, she will start to develop an awareness of her body and the space around her. By crawling or walking over, under, or through everyday objects she will begin to realize the size of her body and the space it takes up. Provide your baby with these experiences by encouraging her to crawl under the table, over a pile of cushions, or through the space between two chairs. The more she explores, the more she will learn about herself and the objects in her world.

69

Fingers and toes

You can play numerous games with your baby's fingers and toes. These touching games all help with the bonding process, while the rhymes that accompany them, such as "This little piggy . . . ," add to the enjoyment. Find time each day to touch and stroke your baby.

70

Bath play

The bath is a good place for your baby to investigate his own body and enjoy feeling the water against his skin. Bath toys can add to the fun. Your baby can float and sink boats, pour and splash water, and squeeze foam toys and sponges. Remember, *never* leave your baby alone in the tub.

Feely things

As your baby gets older, between nine and twelve months, he will love having his own box or bag of things to feel. Make sure that all the items are safe, and include different textures so that he gets to experience the difference between rough and smooth. Select things like squares of velvet, silk, fake fur, a piece of sponge, a rubber ball, and a piece of cardboard. Add new items every now and then so your baby gets a surprise the next time he explores his feely things.

Everyday noises

Teaching your baby about the different sounds she hears every day helps her identify noises and also develops her language skills. Name the object (for example the telephone, doorbell, or television) and, when possible, point to it so she associates the noise with the name of its source. Outside, encourage your baby to identify sounds like birds, airplanes, cars, and buses by pointing to them and telling her their names. In the country, point out farm animals such as hens, sheep, and cows; and identify machinery such as tractors, balers, and combines.

73

Mom's little helper

Although shopping at the supermarket can be a chore for you, it's an adventure for your baby once he has grown a little older (between nine and twelve months). Help develop his language skills by talking about the products you are buying. Tell him their names as you put them in the cart. Ask him to help chose some items.

For example, ask, "Shall we have this bunch of bananas or that one?" This makes him feel involved. Show him how you cross things off your shopping list, and let him hold the list for you as you pack the bags.

Fast-food restaurants

Believe it or not, a fast-food restaurant can be a wonderful learning experience for your baby. He will be fascinated by all the new sights and sounds and intrigued by the families with young children. Add to his enjoyment by making him a simple toy to play with— thread the clean lid of a take-out cup onto a straw and show him how to pull the lid off and put it on again. Then encourage him to try to pull off the lid himself.

75

Ball games

There are endless ball games you can play with your baby, and you can start some of them when he is still very young. Playing with a ball is good for your baby's hand-to-eye coordination and manual dexterity. At first he will enjoy handling a soft ball that has different textures. Later he may enjoy having a number of different-sized balls to play with, in a variety of colors. Show your baby how to drop a ball into a container and listen for the noise it makes. Encourage him to push a ball along the floor as he crawls toward you. Sit him up a little way from you and roll the ball toward him, and teach him how to roll the ball back. Show your baby how to hold the ball in the air and drop it. Encourage him to find it and return it to you before he drops it again. An older baby can learn how to bounce and throw a ball outside. Choose a big, colorful ball that's easy for him to hold.

76

Stimulating crib toys

Your baby will enjoy toys that have strong colors, so choose colorful mobiles and crib toys that will stimulate his interest in the world around him and encourage shape and color recognition. A newborn can focus only on objects about 8–12 inches (20–30 cm) away, so place crib toys and mobiles where he can see them. As he gets older he will get hours of pleasure from an activity center attached to the side of his crib.

77

The great outdoors

Turn a visit to the park into an adventure and help develop your baby's exploration and language skills. Gather together—with help from your little one—some leaves, twigs, stones, and maybe a flower or two. Place all the items in a bucket or box and then, sitting together on a rug or blanket, examine your findings. Encourage your child to hold each item while you tell him its name. Ask him to put each item back into the box as you repeat its name. This is fun for a nine-to twelve-month-old baby, but supervise him to be sure he doesn't put any of the items in his mouth.

78

Black and white

From a very early age your baby will enjoy visually stimulating objects. Even a very young baby is attracted to sharply contrasting colors and patterns. Draw bold designs on white paper with a black felt tip pen and place them around the crib for your baby to look at.

79

Hide and seek

As your baby gets older, he will begin to understand that things still exist even when he can't see them. Show him an object and then hide it under a cloth and ask him if he can find it. If he doesn't get the idea at first, pretend to help him look for it.

Happy Mom, Happy Baby

80

On your bike

A child's seat, fitted to the back of your bike, provides all sorts of opportunities for short trips for you and your baby—once he is over one year of age. Children under one year may be at risk from shaken baby syndrome. For safety's sake, when you do take your older baby for a ride, he must wear an approved helmet, by law, and you should, too.

81

Time out

Make the most of your baby's morning and afternoon naps by sitting with your feet up and closing your eyes. Don't worry about the time of day or the jobs that need doing, just sit and relax. Even if you can't nod off, you'll feel better for the break.

82

Take your baby jogging

Some all-terrain strollers are designed for joggers. If you enjoyed running before you were pregnant, use a stroller to jog with your baby now. Look for one that isn't too heavy, has large wheels, and has a padded handle that is at a comfortable height when you are running. Some all-terrain strollers have shopping baskets; make sure that the one that you choose won't interfere with your feet when you run. You'll feel great after the exercise and the fresh air, and the change of scene will be good for your baby, too.

83

Water babies

Swimming is a great form of exercise as well as an activity that you and your baby can enjoy doing together. However, you should wait until he has had his first series of immunizations before taking him into a pool. Look for adult-and-baby swimming classes at the Y or a local gym. You'll want to find a class taught by an accredited teacher with adult and child certification. These classes usually include a lot of singing and very simple exercises for your baby to follow while in the water. Alternatively, you may prefer going to a general family session where your partner or a friend can accompany you. Having someone with you will certainly help when it comes to changing your baby after the swimming session, when it is important that he doesn't get cold.

An adult-and-baby swimming class will encourage your baby to

enjoy water and feel confident in it, setting a good
background for swimming lessons when he is

older. Swimming together also gives you the chance to
increase your fitness levels and is a great bonding activity.
Your baby will benefit from increased
coordination, improved sleep
patterns, and a healthy appetite as
well as greater self-confidence.

84

Breast-feeding comfort

Make sure that you have everything you need before you start—not just baby things, but also a drink for yourself, a book if your baby is a slow feeder, and some relaxing music, if you like. Put the answering machine on so that you are not disturbed, then settle down in a comfortable chair, making sure that your back is well supported with cushions. If you feel relaxed while you breast-feed, your baby will sense this and nurse more easily.

85

Breast-feeding in bed

Night feedings can be less disturbing if your partner gets up, changes your baby, and brings her to you in bed. Lie on your side with your legs bent and your head supported on your hand or with pillows. Place your baby on the bed beside you, facing your breasts, then draw her toward you so that she can feed from the lower breast. When she's finished on that side, turn over, taking your baby with you, and offer her the other breast.

Soothing sore nipples

Painful red nipples usually occur because your baby has not taken the nipple correctly. Breast-feeding shouldn't hurt, so if you do experience pain, the first thing you should do is check that your baby has taken all of your nipple and areola—the dark surrounding area—into her mouth. Also make sure that you break her hold on your nipple when you remove your baby from the breast by gently inserting your little finger into her mouth. Sometimes thrush in your baby's mouth affects your nipples, making them sore. This is a yeast infection that will need to be treated with antibiotics. If you suspect thrush, go to the doctor. Often soreness occurs during the first weeks of breast-feeding before the nipples have had a chance to toughen up. It's sometimes soothing to rub a little breast milk into your nipples after each feeding and then allow them to dry naturally. It is important to keep your nipples as dry as possible between feedings—don't leave damp breast pads in your bra—and allow your nipples to air as much as possible. Use plain water to wash, and avoid using scented soaps and creams.

87

Looking good

You may notice that after you have given birth you are losing more hair than usual and that the condition of your hair has changed. Maybe it's drier or more oily than it was during your pregnancy. This is perfectly normal. It happens because your hormones are returning to their prepregnancy levels. It can take up to six months after the birth for your hair to return to its usual condition. This is an ideal time to have your hair cut into a style that requires very little care and looks good without your having to do much to it.

88

Baby products can be good for you, too

Products formulated for your baby's delicate skin can be good for yours, too. Try using baby lotion to remove your makeup. It can also double as a moisturizer or a hand cream. Run out of shower gel? Look no further than your baby's bath soap and, while you're in the shower, wash your hair with baby shampoo. Baby oil, applied after a bath or shower, also moisturizes your skin.

89

Eating well

No matter how tempted you are to diet so that you can return to your prepregnancy shape, remember that eating well is important, especially if you are breast-feeding. While nursing, you will need an extra five hundred to six hundred calories a day. Snack between meals on foods that are high in carbohydrates, protein, and calcium. You may be able to eat what you like and still lose weight, or you may have to wait until after you've finished nursing to lose extra pounds. But no matter what, this is not the time to skip meals.

90

Getting toned up

You can start doing simple exercises as soon as three days
after the birth unless there were complications or you
had to have a Caesarean. The sooner you get back
into some form of exercise routine, the sooner
you will lose any pregnancy flab and the
more energy you will have for your baby.

91

Finding a class

If you lack the discipline to follow an exercise routine at home, look for
a postnatal exercise class. Some classes have a supervised nursery
where you can leave your baby for a short time. It will do you good to
get out of the house for a while and make new friends.

92

Give yourself a speedy pick-me-up

A quick scalp massage relaxes you and relieves tension. Sit in a quiet room without any distractions and, using the fingertips of both hands, make small circular movements on your scalp. Make the pressure firm enough so your scalp moves against the bone as you work your way slowly across your head. When you've finished, take some deep, calming breaths, breathing in through your nose and out through your mouth.

93

Relaxing naturally

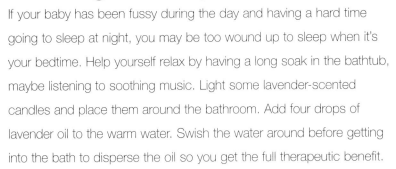

If your baby has been fussy during the day and having a hard time going to sleep at night, you may be too wound up to sleep when it's your bedtime. Help yourself relax by having a long soak in the bathtub, maybe listening to soothing music. Light some lavender-scented candles and place them around the bathroom. Add four drops of lavender oil to the warm water. Swish the water around before getting into the bath to disperse the oil so you get the full therapeutic benefit.

94

Getting back into shape

Avoid full-length mirrors for at least the first six weeks after you've had your baby and forget about trying on your favorite pair of jeans for at least another six weeks. Unless you are very lucky, it will take at least this long to reclaim your prepregnancy shape.

95

Turning your back on housework

Ignore everyday chores and concentrate on important things like caring for your baby and spending time getting to know each other. If anyone has anything to say about the dust building up or the unwashed dishes, smile and hand them a duster or dish detergent.

96

It's not a competition

As a new mother you may find yourself in what feels like a competition with other moms. This is because mothers tend to compare their own performance against that of other mothers, and use their baby's achievements as a measure of their success. The main reason for this is a lack of confidence as well as genuine concern about being a "good" mother. Try not to be upset if your friend's baby seems to be achieving skills long before yours does. Remember that every baby is unique and develops at his or her own rate. If your baby is healthy, you have nothing to be concerned about.

97

Making new friends

It's easy to feel isolated after having a baby, especially if this is your first child and you have recently left a job. Once the visitors have all gone, you may miss friends and colleagues from work, or the support you had from your prenatal group. Some prenatal groups hold reunions for moms and their babies. If yours doesn't, organize one. Alternatively, look for a local mothers group where you and your baby will soon make friends.

Stress management

Motherhood is stressful—you can't get away from this fact. But how you manage your stress can make all the difference to your well-being. There is no right or wrong way—you need to find out what works best for you. A soothing lemon tea is all some moms need; jogging or going to the gym works best for others. No matter what you do, make sure that you find some "me time" each day, even if it's only for a few minutes.

99

Parents are people, too

You may be so tired at the end of the day that you can hardly speak when your partner gets home, never mind being a sparkling conversationalist. But you must make time for each other. You'll be surprised how much good an evening out will do for your relationship. Plan to go out once a week, even if it's for only an hour or two. Hire a trusted person like your mom or best friend to baby-sit, get dressed up, and go out and enjoy being a couple again. Alternatively, just make the effort to have a cozy night in together and really listen to how each other's day has been.

100

Babies have a way of bringing people together

When you are out with your baby, complete strangers will stop and admire him. People will talk to you at the supermarket checkout, on the bus, and in the park. You'll find yourself chatting to other moms at the baby clinic in a way you wouldn't have dreamed of doing before he arrived. Some of these strangers may become new friends, especially the moms who are sharing the same experiences. Suddenly you'll have a whole new social life, thanks to your baby.